D0821685

Manners in the Library

By SHANNON MCCLINTOCK MILLER

Illustrations by KATHRYN DURST

Music by EMILY ARROW

CANTATA
LEARNING

WWW.CANTATALEARNING.COM

CANTATA LEARNING

Published by Cantata Learning
1710 Roe Crest Drive
North Mankato, MN 56003
www.cantatalearning.com

Library of Congress Cataloging-in-Publication Data
Names: Miller, Shannon (Shannon McClintock), author. | Durst, Kathryn,
    illustrator. | Arrow, Emily, composer.
Title: Manners in the library / by Shannon McClintock Miller ; illustrations
    by Kathryn Durst ; music by Emily Arrow.
Description: North Mankato, MN : Cantata Learning, [2018] | Series: Library
    skills | Includes bibliographical references.
Identifiers: LCCN 2017007524 (print) | LCCN 2017018147 (ebook) | ISBN
    9781684100408 | ISBN 9781684100392 (hardcover : alk. paper)
Subjects: LCSH: Library etiquette--Juvenile literature. | Library
    etiquette--Songs and music. | Children's songs, English--United
    States--Texts.
Classification: LCC Z716.43 (ebook) | LCC Z716.43 .M56 2018 (print) | DDC
    395.5/3--dc23
LC record available at https://lccn.loc.gov/2017007524

978-1-68410-304-1 (hardcover)

Book design, Tim Palin Creative
Editorial direction, Flat Sole Studio
Executive musical production and direction, Elizabeth Draper
Music arranged and produced by Emily Arrow

ACCESS THE MUSIC!
SCAN CODE WITH MOBILE APP
CANTATALEARNING.COM

TIPS TO SUPPORT LITERACY AT HOME

WHY READING AND SINGING WITH YOUR CHILD IS SO IMPORTANT

Daily reading with your child leads to increased academic achievement. Music and songs, specifically rhyming songs, are a fun and easy way to build early literacy and language development. Music skills correlate significantly with both phonological awareness and reading development. Singing helps build vocabulary and speech development. And reading and appreciating music together is a wonderful way to strengthen your relationship.

READ AND SING EVERY DAY!

TIPS FOR USING CANTATA LEARNING BOOKS AND SONGS DURING YOUR DAILY STORY TIME

1. As you sing and read, point out the different words on the page that rhyme. Suggest other words that rhyme.

2. Memorize simple rhymes such as Itsy Bitsy Spider and sing them together. This encourages comprehension skills and early literacy skills.

3. Use the questions in the back of each book to guide your singing and storytelling.

4. Read the included sheet music with your child while you listen to the song. How do the music notes correlate to the words of the song?

5. Sing along on the go and at home. Access music by scanning the QR code on each Cantata book. You can also stream or download the music for free to your computer, smartphone, or mobile device.

Devoting time to daily reading shows that you are available for your child. Together, you are building language, literacy, and listening skills.

Have fun reading and singing!

The library is a special place. In a library, you learn about new things. You can meet friends and share **ideas**. The library gives you so much, so be **respectful** when you're there.

Now turn the page to learn about using your best **manners** at the library. Remember to sing along!

LIBRARY

5

Collaborate, **create**, and share.
Show the library that you care.

When we use good manners, it's a safe place to be.
Explore the space. Let your mind be free!

Good manners mean we treat things right,
even when they're out of sight.

Take books home, then bring them back.

Magazines go in the rack.

Use a **device** to study and play.
You can learn in a cool, new way.

TABLET CHECKOUT

Technology is so much fun.

Be sure to store it when you're done.

Collaborate, create, and share.
Show the library that you care.

When we use good manners, it's a safe place to be.
Explore the space. Let your mind be free!

Be kind and offer to help out.

Laugh and share. Get your wiggles out!

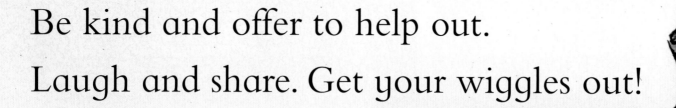

Use your heart to guide your words.
Then your ideas are always heard.

Treat others with respect and love.
Remember not to tease or shove.

Make new friends and collaborate.

Ideas are for sharing. Create! Create!

Collaborate, create, and share.
Show the library that you care.

When we use good manners, it's a safe place to be.
Explore the space. Let your mind be free!

Collaborate, create, and share.

Show the library that you care.

When we use good manners, it's a safe place to be.

Explore the space. Let your mind be free!

21

SONG LYRICS
Manners in the Library

Collaborate, create, and share.
Show the library that you care.
When we use good manners,
    it's a safe place to be.
Explore the space.
    Let your mind be free!

Good manners mean we treat things right,
even when they're out of sight.
Take books home. Then bring them back.
Magazines go in the rack.

Use a device to study and play.
You can learn in a cool, new way.
Technology is so much fun.
Be sure to store it when you're done.

Collaborate, create, and share.
Show the library that you care.
When we use good manners,
    it's a safe place to be.
Explore the space.
    Let your mind be free!

Be kind and offer to help out.
Laugh and share. Get your wiggles out!
Use your heart to guide your words.
Then your ideas are always heard.

Treat others with respect and love.
Remember not to tease or shove.
Make new friends and collaborate.
Ideas are for sharing. Create! Create!

Collaborate, create, and share.
Show the library that you care.
When we use good manners,
    it's a safe place to be.
Explore the space.
    Let your mind be free!

Collaborate, create, and share.
Show the library that you care.
When we use good manners,
    it's a safe place to be.
Explore the space.
    Let your mind be free!

Manners in the Library

Kindie
Emily Arrow

Chorus

Col - lab - o - rate, cre - ate, and share. Show the li - brar - y that you care. When we use good man - ners, it's a safe place to be. Ex - plore the space. Let your mind be free!

Verse

1. Good man - ners mean we treat things right, e - ven when they're out of sight. Take books home. Then bring them back. Mag - a - zines go in the rack.

Verse 2
Use a device to study and play.
You can learn in a cool, new way.
Technology is so much fun.
Be sure to store it when you're done.

Chorus

Verse 3
Be kind and offer to help out.
Laugh and share. Get your wiggles out!
Use your heart to guide your words.
Then your ideas are always heard.

Verse 4
Treat others with respect and love.
Remember not to tease or shove.
Make new friends and collaborate.
Ideas are for sharing. Create! Create!

Chorus (x2)

ACCESS THE MUSIC!
SCAN CODE WITH MOBILE APP
CANTATALEARNING.COM

GLOSSARY

collaborate—to work with someone on a project

create—to make something

device—a machine made to do something

explore—to search

manners—the way people act and how they treat each other

respectful—treating others in a kind way

technology—anything that solves a problem

GUIDED READING ACTIVITIES

1. This book teaches you how to have good manners in the library. Can you think of other ways to be respectful and show good manners in the library?

2. The library isn't the only place it is important to have good manners. Can you think of other places where manners are important? How do you show good manners at these places?

3. Draw a picture of you and your friends at your library. Be sure that you are showing good manners.

TO LEARN MORE

Bloom, Paul. *Rules in the Library*. New York, NY: Gareth Stevens Publishing, 2015.

Gassman, Julie. *Do Not Bring Your Dragon to the Library*. North Mankato, MN: Capstone, 2015.

Martin, Isabel. *A Library Field Trip*. North Mankato, MN: Capstone, 2015.

Mortensen, Lori. *Manners Matter in the Library*. North Mankato, MN: Capstone, 2011.